How to Join a Fraternity

Patrick Daley

ISBN: 1475187432
ISBN-13: 978-1475187434

DEDICATION

This book is dedicated to the brothers of Pi Lambda Phi Fraternity.

CONTENTS

CONTENTS

How to Join a Fraternity

INTRODUCTION

I started my website, www.thefraternityadvisor.com, in 2009. Since then, I have received hundreds of questions on how to join a fraternity. This book aims to collect all those answers to give prospective fraternity men the information they need to make an informed choice on Greek Life.

I hope this book helps you find the right fraternity and I hope it helps you get a bid from that fraternity.

Once you are a brother, but sure to check out my other book, THE FRATERNITY LEADER. This book will show you how to make your fraternity the best on campus.

Fraternally,

Pat

HOW TO FIND THE RIGHT FRATERNITY FOR YOU

This step is NEVER done the right way. Nearly everyone who ever joins a fraternity joins the first and only fraternity they were ever introduced to. Circumstance, maybe you lived with a brother in the dorms or knew a brother from home, is what normally introduces a guy to his fraternity. Very little attention is paid to whether or not it is the right one.

This is extremely unfortunate. Joining a fraternity is a lifelong decision. More immediately, this is the group of guys you will be spending the new four years with. It is pretty important you get this right.

On my thefraternityadvisor.com, the most common question I get is how do I quit my fraternity and join a new one. The answer to this question is it is nearly impossible. In order to switch fraternities, you need to get released from your brotherhood commitment from your national fraternity (good luck) and then you need to be accepted by the new fraternity (again good luck). Most of the time this process takes so long it isn't even really worth trying.

The better scenario is you end up in the right fraternity the first time. Follow this advice to ensure you end up in the fraternity where you belong. While this is a tedious process, it will be well-worth it in the long run.

STUDY FRATERNITIES ONLINE

The very first step in this process is doing your homework online.

First, find the webpage of the Interfraternity council (IFC) at your school. The IFC is the governing board for all fraternities on campus. There will be a link to it from the school's Greek Life Page.

Right down all the fraternities and use this list as a place to gather information.

Then, go to the Greek Life page and see what fraternities won awards. See which fraternity was recognized as the top overall chapter the past few years. Also, check to see who did the most community service and who had the best grades. If that information isn't available, email the IFC advisor and ask for it.

Mark down which fraternities were recognized on your list.

Then, go to the universities intramural webpage. Find out which fraternities performed well in athletics. It is important to see who won the major sports (namely flag football, basketball and soccer), but also to see which fraternity participated in the most sports. Most often the participation will be able to tell you which fraternities take athletics seriously.

Again, mark down your findings on your list.

Then, go to each fraternity's website and investigate there. Some will not have updated in a while. While on the surface you would assume this doesn't tell you much, it actually does. It shows which fraternities are on the ball and which ones aren't.

On the website you can find out the size of the fraternity, what the house looks like, what the brothers look like, their national history and beliefs and you should be able to see some pictures of events they had. Pay special attention to the beliefs and history. Every fraternity is founded on certain beliefs and principals. You need to be aware of these to make sure you are at the right place.

Again, mark down your findings.

By now, you are more equipped to make a decision on a fraternity than 95% of guys who rush. However, you can do more.

GET ADVICE FROM THOSE WHO KNOW

On your sheet you should have a few fraternities that pop out at you. You need to find out more about these guys.

First, go to the Greek Life office and ask to speak to the Greek Life Director of IFC advisor. If you are too timid to go in person, send them an email.

Let them know you are interested in rushing, but want to learn more about a few fraternities. Ask them what the fraternities you are interested in have contributed to the university and the community. This is a very direct question that should tell you a lot about the fraternity.

Also, ask if any of the fraternities on your list have been in trouble for any reason. It is very important to know if a fraternity is on probation or has a history of being on probation. You want to avoid those situations.

Don't forget that if you have friends in sororities or friends who are upperclassman – ask them their opinion. The more opinions you get the better.

Finally, remember that you are the one who is making the final decision on what fraternities to visit. Not every chapter will be perfect, and opinions are just opinions. Take all with a grain of salt.

At this point you should have a few fraternities that you want to visit.

CONTACT THE FRATERNITIES YOU LIKE

On the surface this will seem like an awkward step for someone who has never been in a fraternity. You probably have no idea on how to let a fraternity know you are interested in rushing. You also may think it is presumptuous of you to even ask.

However, I promise you with 100% certainty that any fraternity would love to meet you. Fraternities spend thousands and thousands of dollars on rush to find guys like you. If you find them instead of them having to find you, you have done half their job for them. Every fraternity man will be happy about that.

So what you do is send an email to the recruitment chair or president explaining that you are interested in rushing their fraternity. I would tell them your class, and let them know you have heard a lot of great things about their fraternity and you are definitely interested.

Don't overload them with details about you at this point. This can only hurt your chances of getting a bid in the future. Your goal with this email is to get an invite. Less is more in this situation.

If their email address isn't on their website – contact the IFC advisor and ask them for a contact email.

This will get the ball rolling and get you an invite to a rush event.

DON'T RELY ON YOUR HIGH SCHOOL BUDDIES

I was a master recruiter for my fraternity. My strategy was simple. Every year I knew a couple of guys from high school who would be attending my school that were a year or two younger than me. I found out who these guys were the summer before their freshman year.

That summer, I would reach out to them and hang out a couple times. I would help them with any questions they would have and tell them what school was like.

On the first day of school, I would meet them at their dorm room to see if they needed anything and welcome them to campus.

I would also tell them they are coming to the fraternity house later. I would not give them an option of backing out. I would tell them they are hanging out with me. I would also tell him to bring any of his friends.

So then I would show up, pick up the whole gang of them, and take them to the fraternity house. They would have a great time (as if it is possible not to have a great time your first night away from home).

We would get them to commit to attend the first rush event, and before you know it one event turned into two weeks worth of events. My friend and all his buddies would join the fraternity without ever having experienced any other fraternity.

This was a great thing for us, but probably not the best thing for them.

You need to avoid this scenario at all costs. It is great to go your buddy's house on the first night on campus and go to their rush events. However, you need to experience other fraternities to make the best decision.

RUSH MULTIPLE FRATERNITIES

You need to do this. You won't want to, because going to new environments are hard. It is especially hard after you have done it once or twice already.

Again, remember that most of you will be basing your entire college social life on a two week rush period. If you join the only fraternity you ever visit, you aren't making a choice. You are settling. This decision is too important for that.

Because this is so important, you need to rush at least 3 fraternities. I suggest rushing three on the first three nights. You will then have a good idea of which fraternity to eliminate. Then, visit the other two and see where you would be happiest.

A lot of factors will obviously go into that decision. The biggest one is do you actually like the guys? If you do, and seem like a good fit, then you have found the most important criteria for joining.

I cannot over-emphasize the importance of this step. If you mess this one up, you run the risk of joining a fraternity where you won't be happy and you will be stuck. Don't put yourself in that situation. Sure, it might work out, but taking the extra couple nights to compare fraternities will guarantee it will work out.

GET TO KNOW THE OTHER GUYS RUSHING

During rush your obvious focus will be on the brothers. You will focus on getting to know those guys because they are the ones who currently make up the fraternity.

It is just as important to see the caliber of guy they are recruiting. These guys will become your closest friends in school because you will become members of the same new member class. Not only that, you will be in the fraternity for four years with these guys, and will become the same peer group due to your age.

If you don't like these guys, then there is a strong chance that your fraternity experience will be a bust. Also remember that these guys represent who the fraternity will become, which is almost as important as who they are now.

There is one important caveat to this piece of advice though. Be careful not to be overly critical.

When I was going through rush, one of the guys rushing looked like a stoner. He dressed in really dark clothes, and smoked like a chimney. He wasn't the type of guy I wanted to be associated with based on his appearance.

When I got my bid, I thought long and hard about him before I accepted it. I wasn't sure if he was the type of guy I wanted to call my fraternity brother. However, I took a chance and signed.

It was amazing the transformation in this guy once he was in the fraternity. He lost his stoner-wear and assimilated into the group. On top of that, I realized he was a very good athlete and a very good student. He turned out to be exactly the guy I wanted to be associated with, and we became great friends.

The point here is make sure you study the entire recruitment situation. Pay particular attention to the guys who have already accepted bids (they will be wearing pledge pins). You want to make sure you like these guys too before you decide to join.

FRATERNITY IS FOR LIFE

Like I said earlier – the most common question I get on thefraternityadvisor.com is how does someone change fraternities. This is nearly impossible.

Because of that, it is so important you realize that when you join a fraternity, you are joining it for life.

Now granted, the by accepting your bid and becoming a new member you are not making that commitment now.

That commitment is made at initiation. However, you really don't want to be halfway through the new member period and realize that this chapter is not for you. That is a lot of wasted time and effort for a lot of people, including yourself.

GETTING THE APPROVAL OF PARENTS

When I received my bid I asked for a couple days to think about it. The first thing I did was ask my Dad if I could join.

His response was not what I expected. He told me that I'm a man now, and responsible for my own decisions. He would support whatever I decided.

That was the entire conversation. He didn't offer an opinion and didn't push me one way or the other.

As a parent now, I realize that this is the way it should be. Parents raise their kids to make sound decisions when they are adults. While it isn't easy, good parents will trust that their parenting will ensure their kids make good decisions as adults. And when they leave the house at 18 to go to college, they are adults.

That being said, there is also the golden rule – he who has the gold makes the rules. If Mom and Dad are paying for school and you expect them to pay your fraternity dues, then they have every right to voice their opinion.

So, if you are truly interested in joining a fraternity, and you need your parent's approval, how do you get it?

First, realize their concerns. They don't want you flunking out of school. They don't want you falling into the Animal House stereotype of drinking, partying and drugs. They don't want you to be hazed. They don't want you to be stuck in a decision that you made hastily.

You need to alleviate these concerns. You do so by showing your parents the chapter's academic report. This should show your parents that the group you are joining is committed to scholarship. Also, your parents need to realize that joining a fraternity really doesn't have a bearing on your academics. You will have a social life regardless of if you join a fraternity. In the university setting there are plenty of excuses to avoid studying. You have to prove that you are mature enough to realize your responsibilities and that is academics first.

To give your parents a good impression of the chapter you want to join, ask the fraternity if your parents can contact their advisor. Also, they may want to contact the Greek Life advisor on campus. Get the advisors email addresses and let your parents send an email to them. This should help with the drinking, partying and hazing issue.

Finally, you need to prove that you are making a sound decision. If you did your homework like we have already discussed, you will have that information to show your parents. If you ask the right questions (to come in a later chapter) you will have valuable information on exactly why you want to join. Realize that saying you like the guys is never good enough.

The point here is you want to make sure you completely understand your decision, and have all the facts at hand to make sure your parents trust you are making a sound decision.

In the worst case scenario, let your parents know you will try it and get progress reports from your professors in one month. If you are not achieving academically, tell them that you agree to quit the fraternity. This is a mature way to compromise.

QUESTIONS TO ASK

You must be able to carry a conversation during rush. The key to being a good conversationalist is to ask good, open-ended questions. Below are the types of questions you need to ask. Ask these same questions to as many different brothers as possible. One of the beauties of fraternity is that everyone will get something different out of every experience. Getting multiple perspectives will ensure you will get the information you need to select the right fraternity.

1) Question: How much are dues, and where does the money go?

Why you ask: Obviously, you want to know how much dues are. For most first semester freshman, this is an unexpected expense. You need to make sure you are prepared to meet your financial obligation.

More importantly though, you want to understand where the money goes. How much is spent on social? How much is spent on the house? You want to see if you are getting value for your money.

Joining a fraternity is really no different than any other expense you have in life. You need to understand the benefits of fraternity to see if it is worth the cost.

2) Question: How does the fraternity challenge new members?

Why you ask: What you are really asking is does the fraternity haze. However, you can't ask that question during rush. Of course they are going to answer no.

And truth be told, you will not get a complete answer by asking this question. However, you will get some type of insight into the thinking of the chapter when it comes to new members. Again, ask as many brothers this question as possible. By doing so, you will get a bunch of different answers, and should be able to piece together a pretty good picture of what new members will experience.

3) Question: What are the time commitments and mandatory obligations?

Why you ask: You want to know what the expectations are for a new member. If you are to be at the house every day at 6 to serve the brothers dinner, then you probably don't want to be a part of that fraternity. If there are certain events or dates that are mandatory fraternity functions, then it is good to know about it up front. Again, you are just trying to get a complete picture of what the new member period is like.

Also, be sure you don't limit this question to just your new member period. You want to know what the expectations are for brothers too.

4) Question: How many pledges did you have last fall and how many initiated?

Why you ask: This is a great, great question. First, it will tell you if the fraternity is growing or shrinking. For example, let's say you are rushing a 50 man chapter. However, they only initiated 6 guys last semester. That should tell you that something is wrong, and this chapter might be on hard times.

Also, it tells you a ton about the new member program. If the same fraternity in the above example pledged 10 men, but only 6 became brothers something is wrong. That means that 40% of their new member class quit. There has to be a reason for that.

Of course, you need to ask the follow-up question of why these guys quit. Think about it logically for a second though. If guys are quitting, it tells you one of two things. It could mean that the new member program sucks, and the guys didn't want to be part of it any longer. Or it could mean that the new members learned more about the fraternity during the new member program, and for whatever reason decided they didn't want to be part of the organization.

Both of those are huge red flags.

You want to see a fraternity that is growing, and has very few new members quit. If you can find that, chances are you have found a chapter that is winning. You want to be a part of that group.

5) Who many brothers are in the chapter and how old is the chapter?

Why you ask: While on the surface this appears to be basic information, there is really a lot to be learned from the answers.

The age of the chapter is important. An older chapter will have a lot of alumni, and the chances are it will have the resources to accomplish more. Old chapters become old for a reason.

Conversely, young chapters have their benefits as well. Brothers in younger chapters have the chance to establish 100 years of tradition, instead of follow it. Brothers who are there for the early years have the opportunity to mold the fraternity into a legacy they are proud of. This is appealing to a lot of guys, and was one of the biggest reasons I joined my fraternity.

The number of brothers tells you a lot. If the fraternity has a ton of brothers, it obviously means they are pretty successful and have the resources to do many things. That being said, simply due to the law of numbers, your chance of holding major positions is decreased.

Conversely, if the fraternity is below 25 brothers, this should send up a red flag. A fraternity this size is only one bad year from being in big trouble numbers-wise. It is important to ask the age of the brothers. If you are at 25, but have a majority of sophomores and juniors, then it isn't as dire a situation. However, if half the brothers in the fraternity are seniors, you could be walking into a very bad situation. Be very careful.

6) Question: Have you been on probation?

Why you ask: You want to know if the fraternity is in trouble or not. If the fraternity is on probation, they can be one screw up away from being closed down. If you are initiated into a fraternity you are pretty much locked into that fraternity for life. It doesn't matter if the fraternity is closed down the semester after you are initiated. This could mean you never get to experience fraternity while you are in college.

Because of this, you want to know this important detail. If the fraternity did get in trouble, you want to know what they did. Again, the more information you get the better decision you will be prepared to make.

7) Question: Why should I join your fraternity?

Why you ask: This is the most open ended question you can ask. Unfortunately, most brothers are not prepared to answer it.

Nearly every fraternity man when asked this question will tell you that his brothers are his family. He'd do anything for any one of them. Also, they are different than everyone else on campus.

And this answer tells you absolutely nothing.

Your goal here is to learn more about what the fraternity actually does. If you don't get a good answer to this question – ask the following follow-up questions:

- What are the fraternity's goals for the year?
- What events do you have planned?
- Do you have any mixers scheduled?
- Did you have any mixers last year?
- What is the best part of being a brother?
- What do you do that makes you different?

8) Question: What is the chapter GPA and what majors are the brothers?

Why you ask: I hope your primary goal in college is to graduate and prepare you for the real world. Because of this, you want to make sure the fraternity you are about to join has the same goals and aspirations.

Knowing the chapter GPA is important, but isn't very telling. All it takes are a few dud brothers to pull everyone down. However, it is good to know how the fraternity stacks up academically compared to the all-mens and all-fraternity averages.

More importantly though, you want to know what majors the brothers are. Of course, you will get a wide assortment. Chances are that many brothers are in the same major. If this is a field you hope to study, then that is definitely something positive about this fraternity.

Finally, you want to know if the fraternity has GPA standards. Some fraternities force their members to be on probation if their GPA falls below a certain amount. Some will not initiate their new members unless they have a certain GPA. Some won't even bid guys unless they qualify academically. Be sure to know if the fraternity has these types of rules in place.

9) Question: What is the best thing about being a new member?

Why you ask: You are joining a fraternity because it will be the time of your life. Memories that will last you a lifetime will be created because of your membership. Don't forget that when you are asking questions.

It is very easy to lose sight of that because of the fear of the unknown. We all know the horror stories of what brothers do to their pledges. Fortunately, most of that is exaggeration that gives Greek Life a bad name.

So ask the brothers about the fun you are about to have. Get them tell you stories of the great things the fraternity has done in the past. You want to know these things because you will be experiencing them soon enough.

10) Question: What are the rules about living in the house?

Why you ask: The fraternity house is a unique place. It is the center of a fraternity man's world. However, for a lot of brothers, it is a great to place to visit – not live.

You need to know what the expectations are about living in the house. A lot of fraternities make it mandatory that you live in the house for some period of your college career. Others make the dues much more expensive if you don't live in the house. Both situations are not the end of the world, but you need to be made aware of the situation before you join.

Also, it is good to know how rooms are selected. In most cases seniority will determine which brother picks first. Regardless, it is good to get a complete lay of the land.

Finally, be sure to ask how much the rent is, how many brothers live in the house and how many brothers can live in the house. With this information you can do some quick math to see if the house is a financial drain on the fraternity. Don't forget to include utilities when you do this quick math.

If the fraternity is running a huge deficit, be very wary of that fraternity. Chances are they are using their dues to offset the lack of rent income. This means the fraternity operating budget will be severely reduced, and that isn't a good thing for any chapter.

TYPICAL FRATERNITY RUSH TIMELINE

Technically, fraternities can recruit all year. However, 99% of the new members are recruited during rush weeks that occur the first two weeks of the semester.

This two week rush period will be made up of recruitment events that occur just about every night during that two weeks. These events vary dramatically from school to school.

At MIT, it isn't uncommon for fraternities to spend thousands of dollars hosting lavish surf and turf dinners during rush. On the other end of the spectrum, it isn't uncommon for fraternities to host flag football games on the intramural fields.

Fraternities will publish notice of these events on their websites and on flyers.

Fraternities will be motivated to get you to attend as many events as possible if they think you are someone that has the potential to become a new member. It isn't uncommon for someone rushing to attend events nearly every night.

At the conclusion of the recruitment period, the fraternity will decide who they want to give bids to – IE they will decide who to invite into the fraternity. Bids can be given a multitude of ways and a multitude of places. Getting one is a great honor.

After the accepted bids are collected, the recruitment period will end and the fraternity will start its new member process.

It really isn't more complicated than that...

FORMAL AND INFORMAL RUSH

Rush isn't the same at all schools. Most schools probably have an informal rush. This is normally a two week period at the beginning of each semester that is designated as the rush period. The fraternities are then on their own to host events and abide by university rules. The recruits are on their own to find fraternities to rush, and the fraternities are on their own to find guys to rush them.

However, some schools have a much more structured rush. This is formal rush.

Formal rush is typically run by the Interfraternity Council (IFC). The IFC is a governing board of all the fraternities.

IFC will have a designated time for rush (normally a few days to just over a week). They will require the men who are interested in recruitment to sign up through them.

Then, IFC will be responsible for introducing the men to each of the chapters on campus.

They will do this by bussing the recruits to each chapter. The recruits will spend a set amount of time at each fraternity. Obviously, due to the number of chapters that need to be visited, this time isn't lengthy.

The recruits will get to list their preference of fraternities (normally top 3) at the end of this process. Then, on a Bid

Day established by IFC, the recruits will find out what fraternity selected them.

This is pretty much exactly how most sororities choose their members.

So which is better? There is no doubt in my mind that informal rush is much better for the fraternity and the recruit.

Formal recruitment hurts the fraternity and recruit because of several reasons.

First, the fraternity and the recruits don't get to spend much time with the guys they are about to become lifelong brothers with. It kind of cheapens the thought of brotherhood when the decision is made after a 15 minute presentation and 5 minute talk with 2 brothers.

Second, it clearly favors the stronger chapters. Obviously, some chapters will show better than others. The ones that show better will get the majority of the recruits. This will help keep small chapters small, which hurts the entire fraternity community. This also hurts the chances that a recruit joins the fraternity where he is the best fit because he will end up judging the book by its cover.

Third, it eliminates a majority of the recruitment pool. A good portion of the guys who join fraternities never thought they would join one. But they happen to meet a brother who brought them to an informal rush event and next thing you know they are a brother. By relying on guys to sign up for rush, the IFC is restricting the number of potential new members in fraternities when they don't have to.

Fourth, it does the fraternities a disservice by not letting them develop their social skills. Informal rush is hard work. You have to meet a lot of new people, then plan events where you are pitching your vision of fraternity. This teaches a lot of valuable skills that help brothers later in life.

Obviously, you can't do anything about what method your school uses during recruitment. If you find yourself stuck in a formal recruitment system, be sure to focus on the guys in the chapter. Joining a fraternity is about joining a group of guys who will become great friends. If you make that decision based on anything but the friendship aspect, you are setting yourself up for disappointment.

SHOULD YOU RUSH IN THE FALL OR SPRING?

There is a huge difference between fall and spring recruitment.

In the fall, the majority of the guys who join are freshman. They have only been on campus a few days, and know very little about college life in general, much less fraternities.

Also, the brotherhood is much more motivated to recruit in the fall. Because of this, fall recruitment numbers are typically higher than the spring. The brothers will all be back from summer vacation, and will be eager to get back to the fraternity house to see their brothers. It is an exciting time to be around the fraternity house.

For some reason, spring recruitment isn't as successful. I imagine most people who did not join in the fall have made friends and developed lives outside of the Greek community. Because of this, there isn't as big a desire to join a fraternity.

The brothers know that spring rush will not be as successful as the fall rush, so they will not give it the same attention.

Often, spring new members are comprised of guys who became friends with brothers in the fall. These guys have the advantage of having been around the fraternity for a few months, so nothing is too big a surprise.

So the obvious question is which is better. Everything being equal, the fall is unquestionably a better time to join for several reasons.

First, the class will be bigger and this will make everyone more motivated. Again, everyone is just coming back from summer break, and everyone will want to reconnect with the fraternity.

Also, if you are a freshman, everything will be new to you. This means that nothing will be spoiled. If you wait until the spring you will not be as naïve to the fraternity scene. While this will make you less ignorant, it will make it less fun for you. Remember that sometimes ignorance is bliss.

One added benefit that most people forget is that if you join in the fall, you get to be a brother in the spring. Guys who join in the spring have to wait three months to see what fraternity life is really like.

That being said, it is dumb to rush a decision if you are not confident in it. There is nothing wrong with waiting. Remember though, every semester you wait will be a semester lost as a brother. These will be memories lost forever.

DRY RUSH?

Alcohol is prohibited at recruitment events – regardless of whether you are of age or not. It seems like the powers that be believe that students don't make the best decisions while under the influence.

While I am sure most undergraduates don't like this rule, it probably is in their best interest. Joining a fraternity is a life-long commitment. While evaluating a chapter, it is probably best to do so with a clear head.

Regardless, a high percentage of fraternities don't abide by this rule. Most fraternities do not know how to effectively recruit new members, and as a result will turn to alcohol and partying.

What does this mean for you?

Well expect to be offered drinks during recruitment. It is your choice of whether to accept or not.

If you do decide to drink, note that you will be breaking several rules by doing so. Of course, if you do, don't be stupid about it.

If you get caught drinking underage and get in trouble, the incident will eventually be tied back to the fraternity. This will get them in big trouble (which is deserved) but will also probably kill your chances of getting a bid.

Also, do not get stupid drunk. Remember that the brothers are evaluating you. It isn't cool to get stupid drunk and puke or pass out. This will not leave the impression you want to give.

Also, people tend to say dumb things when under the influence. You do not want to offend a brother or a guest because you could not control your mouth. Don't be that guy.

WHAT ARE RECRUITMENT EVENTS EXACTLY?

Fraternities predominately use rush events as their recruitment tool of choice. Essentially, these events will have the goal of showing the perspective new member a great time and promote interaction with the brothers.

Typical events fall in a few categories.

There will be athletic events such as playing basketball or flag football. Obviously the intent here is to see if any of the new members are athletes. Even if you aren't an athlete, it will benefit you to show up. If you participate, you will be seen as a good sport (especially if you can laugh at yourself). If you decide to just hang out, you will get valuable time with brothers who will doing the same thing.

There will be obviously be several social events. There are an unlimited number of options here, really too many to list. The intent here is to have a good time, and see if you are a good fit with the brothers.

There will be Greek events. These could be mixers with sororities, or invite only dinners with the brothers. You need to make it a point to attend these type of rush events. This will be your best exposure to fraternity life. Let's face it, you will partake in social and athletic events regardless of whether you join a fraternity or not. You know if you already like those. What you don't know is what it is like being in a fraternity. Here is your chance to see what it is like.

Finally, some fraternities will have rogue events. This essentially boils down to stuff the fraternity isn't supposed to do. This could be unsanctioned parties or strippers. These obviously won't be published on a rush flyer, and if you find out about them that is a good sign that the fraternity is interested in you.

Again, be smart if you find yourself in those situations. The fraternity is committing a clear violation of university rules, and could pay dearly for getting caught. They are also showing a disregard for those rules, which should raise a red flag. If they are a top-notch fraternity, you have to wonder why they resort to such tactics.

COST AND TRANSPORTATION

I realize that rush is an intimidating experience. There are basic questions about how everything works. Two of those questions pertain to cost and transportation.

You probably want to know how much rush is going to cost you.

Rush is free for recruits. All the event costs, food and fun will be paid for by the fraternity.

That being said, don't be an idiot. Bring a few bucks with you just in case you need it. However, don't expect to spend it.

The reason everything is free is because fraternities dedicate a large portion of their budgets for their recruitment periods. Fraternities need new members to survive, and thus spend a significant amount in recruitment.

Another question is about transportation. Fraternities realize that freshman do not have transportation, and are willing to pick you up to make a rush event and drive you home after. All you need to is ask for a ride and you will get one.

DEALING WITH MEETING A LOT OF NEW PEOPLE

Rush will be pretty crazy. Like stated earlier, some brothers (strangers at this point) will pick you up and take you to the fraternity house. There you will be introduced to more brothers (more strangers) and the other guys who are rushing (more strangers).

Essentially you will be in a position where you will meet a ton of new people in a very short period of time. Remembering names will be a problem.

Do your very best to remember someone's name when possible. There are hundreds of tricks to do this. One way it to say the person's name immediately after they tell it to you.

What I suggest doing is try to remember something about the person. For example, maybe the brother will tell you he went on a summer vacation to Vegas. Remember him as Joe, the guy who went to Vegas. This association has helped me through the years.

Also, don't forget that they are going to have a tough time remembering your name. You are probably one of a lot of guys rushing. It is natural for them to get mixed up too.

In this type of situation, a gentleman will always remind the person he is talking to his name. For example, when someone walks up to you, say "I'm Doug if you don't remember". They will ALWAYS say they do remember, even if they don't. Regardless, you gave them the opportunity to save face while telling them your name. It's always a classy move.

On the flip side, if you don't remember their name, politely ask them to remind you. Say, "I'm sorry, I have met a lot of people today and I forgot your name. Could you remind me?" Said this way no harm will be done.

Always ask for this reminder when the conversation starts. There is nothing more awkward than having a 20 minute conversation with someone, and not knowing their name the entire team. After 20 minutes you can't go back and ask them. You are kind of stuck at this point.

RUSHING OUTSIDE RUSH

There is part of rush that will take you by surprise. You will actually be rushed outside of the fraternity rush events.

This can happen a bunch of different ways. It can be as common as a brother dropping by your dorm room to talk or having a brother invite you to lunch.

One rush technique I had was to take a perspective new member to play golf. This forced us to hang out for a few hours without distractions. It was a great way to really get to know a guy and see if he was a good fit for the fraternity. Also, I have always believed you can learn about a guy on the golf course.

Obviously, if the fraternity is making an effort to rush you outside their rush events, they have an interest in you. Don't blow off their advances if you are interested in the fraternity.

1. Questions You Will Be Asked During Recruitment:

Fraternity recruitment is intimidating. It is never comfortable to be introduced to 30, 50 or 100 new guys. I get that.

There is a way to make it less stressful for you. That way is actually spending some time thinking about how you will answer certain questions you will be asked by the brothers during rush.

Here are some common questions you can expect a brother to ask you during rush:

- Do you plan on joining a fraternity this semester?
- Why do you want to join a fraternity?
- What do you want to get out of being in a fraternity?
- What talents can you bring to the fraternity?
- What are the accomplishments you are most proud of?
- How do your parents feel about you participating in rush?
- What do you like to do?
- What sports do you play?

When you formulate your answers, remember why they are asking you these questions. They want to see if you are a good fit for their fraternity. They are looking for guys with good grades, leadership potential, athletic skill as well as someone who they want to be friends with. The more of those boxes you can check the better. A good way to do that is by making sure you are prepared to answer these questions.

COMMON MISTAKE 1

WAITING FOR RUSH TO COME TO YOU

The first few weeks of any semester is a blur. Everything is new. You have new classes. You probably have new roommates. If you are a freshman, then you really don't have your inner circle of friends established. And then rush happens.

It is very common to want to rush, but wait for a fraternity to recruit you. This is the best strategy to make sure you slip through the cracks.

If you want to rush, your best bet is to make the first move. You need to find the fraternities that you are interested in, and contact them.

They will be more than eager to hear from you and will definitely make sure you attend a rush event.

Remember that rush is typically only two weeks. If you hesitate at all, chances are it will be over before you know it. Don't let this fantastic opportunity pass you by.

COMMON MISTAKE 2

BEING TIMID

Fraternity rush is a crazy time. Think about it from the brother's perspective. They have just got back from either summer or winter break. They are looking to catch up with their best friends (their fraternity brothers) to see what happened over the break. But then, they have rush tossed in and that only adds to the chaos.

During rush these brothers will be introduced to quite possibly a couple hundred guys. Again, this all happens in two short weeks.

If you are timid, then there is a good chance you won't be remembered. If you aren't remembered, then you will have a difficult time getting a bid.

Don't be the wall flower that sees your opportunity pass you by. Be confident and talk to the brothers. Have meaningful conversations. This is the best way to be remembered.

COMMON MISTAKE 3

VISITING ONLY ONE FRATERNITY

I understand why this happens. You rush a fraternity, have a great time and are invited back. Because you had such a great time, you go back for a second rush event. Before you know it, you have fallen in love with the fraternity and there is no time to visit anyone else. But let me ask you...

Would you marry the first girl you ever met? Would you buy the first car you ever drove? Of course you wouldn't.

However, this is very common when joining a fraternity.

Think about this one for a second. You are going to join an organization with a lifelong commitment. The fraternity will be the center of our entire existence during the next four years of college. Why in the world would you not at least check out another fraternity to get a comparison?

Do yourself a favor and visit at least two fraternities during rush. I recommend three, but you need to check out two at a minimum.

There are some very clear benefits to visiting multiple fraternities, but also some not-so-clear ones. Obviously, you will now have a reference to compare fraternities. This is very important.

In addition though, the brothers of the both fraternities will now know you are rushing multiple houses. This will make you more desirable in the eyes of both fraternities.

Also, eventually you will become a brother in a fraternity. Having the experiences of rushing multiple houses will give you a good idea of what to do, and what not to do. This will make you more valuable during recruitment.

COMMON MISTAKE 5

BEING RUDE

My fraternity hosted a rush event one semester where we invited potential new members to a minor league baseball game. I met a guy who was interested in attending the rush event, and I picked him up at his dorm room.

I explained to him that the fraternity is covering the cost of the event, and if there is every anything he needs to let me know.

At the game, you would have thought I was his waiter. He said he was hungry and wanted a hot dog. So I got him a hot dog. Then he wanted nachos, so I got him nachos. Then peanuts and on and on....

I really felt he was taking advantage of the fraternity's hospitality. However, I was willing to cut him a break because we obviously were recruiting him.

Another brother mentioned to me that he hadn't even thanked us once after dropping him off at his room after the event. I didn't realize it at the time, but he was right.

This guy did attend another rush event or two, but he turned off so many brothers by his rudeness that first night that he never got a bid.

During another rush, there was a guy who was rushing a couple different fraternities. He insisted on comparing everything about the different fraternities, and made no secret of his opinions.

For example, he told us that our house wasn't as nice as the house of another fraternity. He also commented that our intramural teams weren't as good.

Simply put, this guy was rude as hell and we were put off by him. We realize he was comparing us, but he should have kept his negative opinions about us to himself. You wouldn't walk up to a girl and tell her that her eyes were pretty but her nose was ugly would you? Same thing here.

Don't forget that fraternities spend a ton of money on recruitment. You shouldn't feel bad about it or feel the need to chip in. The reason they spend the money is to meet guys like you. But you should always be appreciative and thank them for having you as their guest. You should also follow common etiquette and not say anything negative about anyone. If you can remember those two things, then you will likely avoid this common problem.

COMMON MISTAKE 6

NOT FITTING IN

I am not a believer in political correctness. I think it cripples people by avoiding reality. So I am going to give it to you straight.

Not everyone deserves a trophy, everyone does not have to be accepted everywhere and not everyone is going to like you.

What this means for fraternity rush is there are going to be chapters out there that don't want you. It could be for real reasons like they think you are a jerk, or it could be for bad reasons like they don't think you have the right 'look' for their chapter.

When these situations present themselves, it is always best just to move on.

I hear of so many guys who can't take the hint and they insist on fighting a losing battle trying to get a bid from these chapters. What they don't realize is that it is never going to happen.

Of course, I always wonder why the want the bid so bad. Why would anyone want to be part of a fraternity that doesn't want them?

During rush, if you fear that you might not fit in, ask a brother. Ask him if you are under consideration for a bid and if he thinks you would be a good fit with the brothers.

If he tells you yes, then you are probably good. If he isn't confident in his answer, or defers it by saying someone else is in charge of making that call, then that is a red flag.

Rush is short. You are going to have to make judgment calls. If you feel like you aren't a good fit, cut your losses and find a fraternity where you are a better fit. While it hurts to not be accepted now, that pain is temporary and pales in comparison to not being in a fraternity or being in the wrong fraternity.

COMMON MISTAKE 7

NOT MAKING TIME FOR RUSH

Rush is short. There is a ton packed into a very small window of time. If you want to get a bid and join a fraternity, you are going to have to bite the bullet and make the time sacrifice during rush.

Not doing so gives the wrong impression. The brothers will assume you aren't interested if you don't accept their invitations to rush events. And remember that they are juggling dozens of guys during rush. You will quickly get crossed off the list after not accepting a few invites.

Not making time for rush obviously looks bad on you, but it also hurts you in the long run. You need this time to evaluate if the fraternity is right for you or not. This means you need to attend as many events as possible and meet as many brothers as possible. I cannot overstate how significant being in a fraternity will impact the rest of your college career.

You need to give the decision the time and diligence it deserves to make sure you make an informed choice.

COMMON MISTAKE 8

NOT LEAVING CONTACT INFO

On the surface, you probably believe that the fraternity you are rushing is a well-oiled machine. I hate to break it to you, but that probably couldn't be further from the truth.

Fraternity rush is like a duck on the water. On the surface everything looks fine and calm. Under the water though the duck is paddling like hell.

Because of this, it is not uncommon for stuff to get lost.

In fact, disaster struck my fraternity one fall recruitment period. We had guys fill out contact sheets the when they arrived at the house. This is how we kept track of who attended the event and this is where we kept their contact information.

Of course, we lost the folder with everyone's contact information. There were some very high potential guys that we never saw again because we didn't know how to get in touch with them.

Now, I realize this was in the days before Facebook and cell phones (damn I'm old), but the reality exists that there is the potential that your info could slip through the cracks.

The solution to this problem is to make absolutely sure that the fraternity has your contact info. Be sure to fill out a rush sheet or send an email to the recruitment chair. It also isn't a bad idea to share contact info with a brother or two.

If you don't get invited back to a rush event, send the recruitment chair an email letting him know you had a good time and wonder when the next rush event is. If he responds, it means you fell through the cracks and it is a good thing you went the extra mile to stay in touch.

If he doesn't respond see #6 above.

COMMON MISTAKE 9

GIVING MIXED SIGNALS

Every so often there will be a strange type of guy who rushes a fraternity. He will act like he doesn't want to be there. He won't ask questions about the fraternity, and he won't go out of his way to meet the brothers.

In turn, the brothers will be confused by this guy. He will show the initiative by showing up to the rush events, but he won't do anything to show he has any interest in the fraternity.

So when it becomes time to make a decision on whether the guy should get a bid or not, most brothers will not be in favor because the guy just didn't seem interested.

Don't be the brother who gives mixed signals. If you want to be in a fraternity, then ask questions about it and act like you want to be there.

The last thing you want it the brothers misinterpreting your body language and crossing you off because of it.

COMMON MISTAKE 10

BLINDLY ACCEPTING A BID

Most guys are naïve during the rush process. They don't realize that the guys who the fraternity wants to become new members are invited with a bid.

A bid can be given any number of ways. Nearly all instances involve a group of brothers presenting a formal card (bid) for the guy to sign. If he signs, he is signifying that he wants to become a member of the fraternity.

Because most guys are naïve about this process, they are swept up in emotion when the time comes and they will immediately sign the bid. Almost immediately doubt creeps into their head of whether or not they did the right thing.

Don't be this guy. If you know you want a bid and you completely understand what you are getting yourself into, then by all means sign it.

But if you have some doubt, or have some more questions, politely tell the brothers that this is a great honor, but you'd like some time to think about it.

Of course, the brothers will press you and ask you if you have any questions. If you have any – ask. However, if you just want some time to think about it, let them know that you think you have all your questions answered, but you just need a night to sleep on it.

This will ensure you make a sound decision and will also make sure you don't become the guy who signs his bid then flakes out.

HOW TO GET A BID

To determine how to get a bid, you first need to understand what you bring to the table.

You must always remember that fraternity recruitment is a two way street. It isn't only about learning about the fraternity, they want to learn about you as well.

One of life's most important lessons is that if you want to get what you want, you have to give what someone else wants.

For you, this means to get a bid you must be able to give the fraternity what they want in a new member. Below are seven things the fraternity is looking for in new members:

1) Most importantly, fraternities are looking for people they like. Fraternities are membership organizations that are based on friendship. If the brothers don't like you, then nothing else really matters.

2) Fraternities are always looking for guys who can recruit new members. Fraternity recruitment is the most difficult part of the life of a chapter. Unfortunately, there just aren't that many guys who are good at it. If you can show a fraternity that you can help them recruit, that will be a big feather in your cap.

3) Fraternities are looking for good athletes. Fraternity intramurals are important. Winning at fraternity intramurals is more important. Fraternities are always looking for guys who can help their chapter win.

4) Fraternities are looking for good students. Chapter GPA is important. Having a brother who takes his studies seriously is an asset to the fraternity. A fraternity cannot get enough of these guys.

5) Fraternities are looking for leaders. One of the great things about fraternity is chapter leadership changes every year, if not sooner. This means that the fraternity will need guys to quickly step up into leadership roles. It is not uncommon to be a new member as a freshman, and be president at the beginning of your junior year.

6) Fraternities want guys who are involved on campus. Fraternity men are well rounded, and strong chapters are proud when their brothers hold leadership positions outside the fraternity. Brothers who are RAs, in student government and are varsity athletes bring great credit to the fraternity and are always in high demand.

7) Fraternities like guys who are popular with girls. If you have this trait, you instantly gain credibility in the eye of the fraternity. The reason for that is every fraternity knows how important it is to have girls around. It is critically important that they have a positive opinion of the brotherhood. If you are popular with girls, you need

to be able to show the chapter this by bringing your friends or girlfriend by the house.

Your goal during fraternity rush is to show the brothers that you possess as many of these qualities as possible. This is how you get a bid.

WHAT TO WEAR

I know the stereotype. Fraternity guys wear Polo, Lacoste and Sperrys. They all look the same, so your thought is that is how you should look.

This is the part where I want to say wear whatever you want and if they don't like it they can kiss your ass. However, your goal is to get a bid and there is a lot of truth in 'birds of a feather flock together'.

My advice is to do your best to assimilate. You don't have to be 100% fratastic by any means. But you should dress so you fit in.

Fortunately, this isn't difficult and shouldn't cost a fortune. Wear a polo (the style, not the brand) or a button-up shirt. Avoid brand logos on your clothes unless it is one of the popular ones. Wear khaki pants or shorts. Avoid wearing tennis shoes.

If you can follow those few guidelines, you will fit in. If you are really not confident in your appearance, ask a trusted girl friend to help you out. Or, take notice of what the guys in the fraternity are wearing, and try to closely match it.

You are probably wondering why this is important. For one, your appearance will be the first impression someone has of you. In a fraternity setting this means that a bunch of people will get their first impression of you at the same time.

You don't want to be labeled as the guy with the ugly shirt or jean shorts guy.

You want what you wear not to distract from who you are. You want impressions to be formed by the conversations you have with the brothers. By limiting unnecessary distractions, you can ensure that will happen.

HOW TO ACT

I know you have an image of how a fraternity man should act in your head. Whatever image you have, get it out of your head.

There is no cookie-cutter answer to how a fraternity man should act. Men in fraternities are as diverse as any group on your campus.

The secret here really isn't about how you act, it is about how the brothers in the fraternity act.

My advice is for you to be yourself. Act how you would normally act. I would hope that is as a gentleman with a respect to common courtesies and manners. Regardless, it is critical that you be yourself.

At the same time, observe how the brothers are active. You should be able to get a good sense of if these are guys that you really want to associate with the rest of your college career.

There is one critical reason why you want to be yourself during rush. I cannot overstate the importance of this point.

You want the brothers to like you for who you are. You don't want them to like fake you. You need to be honest with who you are here because the truth will come out eventually. The very worst thing that can happen to you is you pretend you are someone you aren't just to fit in, and then you become a brother.

As a brother, you find out that you really don't have as much in common with the brothers or worse don't even like them. They may feel the same way about you. At this point though both of you will have invested so much time in each other it is tough to cut ties (kinda like a bad marriage).

Save yourself a ton of trouble and be yourself during rush. Find guys who you fit in with, and join that fraternity. Remember your goal is not to get accepted into any fraternity. Your goal is to find and get accepting into the fraternity where you belong.

BRING OTHER GUYS OUT

Like I have mentioned a couple times, fraternity recruitment is tough. It seems like 30 fraternities are all recruiting from the same pool, and that makes it harder for everyone.

Probably the easiest way to get in the good graces with a fraternity is to help them recruit guys during rush. If you can invite a few of your friends to attend a rush event, this will earn you some serious recognition from the fraternity.

When I was going through rush, I recruited a good friend of mine from high school to rush with me. He was a high potential individual and I know the chapter was impressed that I brought him out. I had found a guy that they would have never had a chance with because they didn't know him. This showed the brothers that I had what it takes to contribute.

You need to do the same thing. There has to be at least someone you know who would want to go to a fraternity rush event. It is not your job to convince him to join. That is the fraternity's job. However, if you can bring him out and give the fraternity the opportunity, it will bode well for your chances of getting a bid.

HOW TO ACT AROUND GIRLS

If the fraternity is any good, there will be girls around during rush. It could be girlfriends or just friends of the chapter. Here are a few rules to remember to make sure you act appropriately.

1) Don't hit on any girls. Nothing good will come of this. First, you don't know what relationships exist. You could be hitting on a girlfriend (I've seen it happen) or you could end up hitting on a girl that a brother likes. If you do the latter, chances are that brother will immediately trash you because they will see you as competition for the girl. Do not, under any circumstances, hit on any girls at the house.

2) Always be a gentleman. Don't swear or tell crass stories around girls. Don't forget that they are forming an opinion of you as well. This opinion will get back to the brothers. Make sure it is a positive one

3) Don't ignore the girls. If you read #1 and #2 above, and think your way of staying out of trouble is just to avoid the girls, think again. If you avoid them, the brothers will think you are afraid of girls. This will negatively impact their opinion of you.

4) To interact with girls, ask a lot of questions. This is the key to conversation. Also, it is interesting to get their perspective on the fraternity.

WHAT HAPPENS IF YOU DON'T GET A BID?

This is a common question I get on thefraternityadvisor.com. Here is typically how the situation goes down:

A guy goes to a rush event or two. Falls in love with the fraternity and is convinced that he wants to join. However, he stops getting invited to rush events.

Thinking that there is an oversight, he calls the fraternity to see what is up. He gets blown off (often more than once).

He then writes me whether or not he should continue trying to rush the same fraternity.

The answer is very obvious, but there is a lesson to be taught here. So I ask the guy the following questions:

Why did you like the fraternity?

What type of things does the fraternity do?

Did you feel like you made a connection to any of the brothers?

How do you know this fraternity is the right one for you?

After I ask these questions, the guy will often realize that he did not have a very good grasp on the fraternity at all.

He was swept up in the moment and wanted a bid because that is what is supposed to happen.

Not getting a bid could be the best thing that ever happened to him. If he didn't get a bid, that means the brothers did not think he was a good fit in their group. This is not a knock on the guy, just a fact of life. You aren't going to fit in everywhere.

A worse scenario would be to get a bid from a fraternity where you aren't a good fit, only to realize it a couple semesters into you college career. That is miserable.

If the fraternity doesn't think you are a good fit – then take it at face value and move on. Go somewhere where you are wanted. Go somewhere where the brothers are falling all over themselves to get you to become their brother. This is the place you are supposed to be.

RUSH BEHIND THE SCENES

I understand where you are at. You don't know anything about Greek Life, much less fraternity life. Knowing how fraternity rush works behind the scenes would probably help you understand the process a little better.

Unfortunately, nearly every fraternity does it a different way. Fortunately, the basic premise is about the same.

A brother will be elected to be the recruitment chair or VP during normal fraternity elections. This is a critical role for the fraternity because if they don't get new members, then the fraternity will suffer extreme consequences. If the recruitment drought is severe enough, they could cease to exist.

This recruitment chair is given a budget to spend on rush. Of course, the budget depends on a lot of factors. Rest assured though that this is a pretty healthy line item in the overall chapter budget.

The recruitment chair will spend that money on recruitment events to try to entice outsiders to join. A schedule will typically be made several months in advance to make sure that the venues the brothers want are available.

Also during this time, the brotherhood will make a list of guy who they think has high potential to become a member. This could be friends of brothers or guys they knew from high school. They will really focus on these guys because logic states that they should be the easiest to get to join.

Obviously, it is key to get on that list. That is why I recommend reaching out to chapters you are interested in early. If you can get your name on that list early, eventually they will put a name with a face and this will increase your chances of getting a bid.

During rush events, as many brothers as possible will try to get to know you. This is because the brotherhood will typically have a vote on whether or not to give you a bid.

Now, I imagine you think this is like Animal House where they put your picture up on a wall and all the brothers moan and groan over it. That would be funnier than how it actually typically happens.

What happens is your name will be brought up. Half the guys in the room won't remember you or won't know you. Some won't care. The one or two guys who you had a conversation with will give their thoughts on you, meaning they are pretty much making the call on you.

He will either say you are cool – and then you are in. Or he will say you are rough around the edges – but have potential. Then you are in. Or he will say you are a tool – and then the fun happens.

Often, in the quest to keep recruitment numbers high, a brother will come to the rescue of the tool rushee. He will say that sure he is a tool now, but so were brothers X, Y and Z when they rushed. Then everyone will have a good laugh.

Then they will say you deserve a chance and if they don't like you then they will kick you our during the pledge period.

After the brothers decide who they want to give bids to, they will assign brothers to give them. Typically the president and rush chair have a role. Most often they will select brothers who they think have the best shot at landing your signature.

The bid can be given at the house or in your dorm. All chapters do it different.

Once bids are accepted and rush is over, the chapter will have a pinning ceremony which will mark the start of the new member period.

It really isn't more complicated than that.

BONUS SECTION

HOW TO START A FRATERNITY

If you have read my bio on thefraternityadvisor.com, you will see that I have accomplished nearly everything possible in a fraternity on a local, national and university level. I have won every significant award, and held every major leadership position.

However, there is one fraternity experience that I wish I would have had. I wish I would have started my own fraternity from scratch. This would have been an incredible challenge, but would have been incredibly rewarding. That would have been an awesome way to leave my legacy, but I never even realized I had the chance.

If you are reading this, then you understand this possibility. You realize there is an opportunity to leave your mark on the campus. I hope you take advantage of this opportunity.

This report will show you the details on how to start a fraternity in the most efficient way possible. By no means is this the only way, but this is how I would do it. It will also help explain some of the details about fraternity life that you probably don't know.

Again, I wish you the best of luck in this challenge. Remember that the biggest rewards are always as a result of the biggest challenges. I wish you the best on your journey.

Starting an Interest Group

Starting an interest group is the most difficult part of this entire process. If you can establish a solid interest group, then everything else will work out. It is imperative that you do this right.

First off, you have to establish your core group. These are going to be the four or five good friends you have that want to start the fraternity with you. You really can't proceed until you have this core group.

Once you have your core group established, each of you needs to write a list of all the people you know who you would want to be in your fraternity. Make sure you don't leave someone off the list because you don't know them that well or because you don't think they'll join. Worry about that later.

After compiling your lists, you should have a pretty healthy pool of potential guys. Next, highlight the guys with the highest potential. These could be guys you think would join, or guys who you think would make really awesome brothers if they did. Then, each member of the core group needs to focus on recruiting these guys.

The recruitment at this stage is pretty informal. You just need to let the guy know of your intentions, and ask if he wants to explore starting the new fraternity with you.

Make sure he realizes that he isn't being asked to join a fraternity, but to help you start one. Make sure he realizes that he will be a founding father of something that will last for years after he graduates.

Once you have added these guys to your core group, have the new guys make their list. Have them highlight the guys with high potential, and be sure those guys get brought into the fold as well.

It shouldn't take long before you get a core group of about 20 guys. Once you get to 20 or so guys, you will have formed a really solid interest group. If you get here, your chances of starting a fraternity are very high.

The First Fraternity Meeting

So you have your initial interest group. You have 20 or so gung-ho guys who are interested in starting a fraternity. Next you need to figure out what your fraternity is going to be all about.

Get the guys in your interest group in a room, and have an open conversation of what everyone is looking to get out of the fraternity.

There are going to be some guys who are going to want to party like rock stars. There are going to be others who want to meet girls. Others will want to improve in academics. Others will look to form a solid network for life after college. Some will look to strengthen religious beliefs. Others will be primarily for guys of certain majors. You get the idea.

Regardless, it is important that the group understands the purpose of the fraternity they are about to start. Once you do this, you will be able to communicate your vision to others.

The Second Fraternity Meeting

The next thing you have to determine if you want to join a national fraternity. This conversation should be had in a separate meeting.

Now, I know there are those of you out there that say you don't want to associate with a national fraternity. You don't want big brother looking over your shoulder and telling you want to do. I understand your point, but let me explain why that is the wrong choice.

The biggest reason is insurance. If someone is hurt or dies at the fraternity house someday, you do not want to be held liable. National fraternities have national policies that protect their members. This is absolutely huge.

Think about it. Your fraternity will have crazy, throw down parties someday. People will make bad decisions and dicey situations will result. Do you really want to be fearful that someone could sue you for someone else's bad decisions just because you were in the same fraternity? This alone is a good enough reason to affiliate with a national fraternity.

Another huge benefit is a national fraternity will help your new chapter when it gets in trouble someday. It might not be for years down the road, but someone will break a university rule eventually. If you are a chapter of a national fraternity, they will come to the fraternity's aid in this situation.

First, nationals will meet with the chapter and resolve that issue. Their goal is to ensure the longevity of the chapter. Then, they will meet with the university in your defense. If you are looking to leave your legacy, don't you want to know that someone has a vested interest in making sure your chapter doesn't die? A national fraternity gives you that reassurance.

Another benefit is that they will help you provide structure to the fraternity. A fraternity comes with a ton of stuff that you just don't want to deal with. You don't want to spend your time designing crests and pins. You don't want to write pledge manuals and rituals. Those are necessary parts of a fraternity, but not a lot of fun to create.

Also, once you start a fraternity you will not have any idea of what you are doing. Wouldn't it be helpful to have a trusted resource helping you out? That is the assistance a national fraternity would provide.

A final benefit is it is pretty cool to be a part of a national fraternity. You will get to benefit from the years of history of the fraternity. The fraternity will have some pretty famous alumni, and they will instantly become your brothers. You will be invited to national conventions where you will meet other brothers from other schools. You will be welcome at any chapter house in the country of your fraternity. Also, these will be the people who recognize *you* when your chapter becomes a success.

There is a negative to being part of a national fraternity though. You will have to pay for your insurance and dues. Both aren't cheap. Every fraternity is different, but it will probably be a couple hundred bucks a brother per year.

Realize though that no one will be telling you what to do. More than likely, your national headquarters will be miles away from your school, and the only time someone will step foot on your campus is for a visit from a leadership consultant. Don't let this irrational fear scare you.

It really is a no-brainer to join a national fraternity. Which leads us to the next question…

How to Pick a National Fraternity:

First off, go here http://www.nicindy.org/about/ to see which national fraternities exist.

This is a list of all the national fraternities out there. Their names are hyperlinked, so you will be able to visit their websites.

Here is what I would look for when trying to determine which one is right for you:

1) Where are most of their chapters located? You want to be close to other chapters if possible. Also, you need to make sure they don't have a chapter already on your campus.
2) Who are their famous alumni? While it really doesn't matter, it is pretty cool to have famous alumni.
3) How many chapters have they started in the past few years? This should be easy to see from their chapter roll and shows if they are dedicate to expansion.
4) How many leadership consultants do they have on staff? These guys are going to be the ones who assist you in getting the fraternity off the ground.
5) And most important, what are the core values of the organization? You obviously want one that aligns with your viewpoints.

You should have a good idea at this stage of who you are interested in. Now you need to prove that you are a good candidate.

How to Earn the Approval of the University

Let's recap where you are at this stage. You have formed an interest group of about 20 guys. You have narrowed down the list of fraternities you want to associate with. Now you want to talk to the university to get their approval before you move forward.

The place to start is with the Director of Greek Life. Set up an hour appointment with him. Be sure to bring one or two other members of your core group. You guys are looking to prove that you have what it takes to start a new fraternity, so wear suits to the meeting. You want the director to realize you are serious.

At the meeting, let the director know that you would like to know how to start a new fraternity on campus. Let them know you have formed an interest group of 20 men, and you have narrowed down the list of fraternities you are interested in. Let him know what those are.

The first question they will ask is what are the fraternities that are already on campus not offering that you are looking for? This is a logical question.

At this point, explain to him that there is nothing wrong with the fraternities that already exist. Explain to him that you realize that they do a lot of good for the university community, and that is a big reason why you want to join the Greek community.

However, your group of guys is looking to start something new, something based on the values you established in your first meeting. Let him know that you have formed a group with strong leadership potential, and the guys want to leave the university with a positive legacy.

To be honest, you will go back and forth several times with the director. They will continually try to convince you to join a fraternity that already exists. They know it is difficult to start a fraternity, and at this stage they will not be sure you have what it takes to pull it off. However, having an interest group of 20 guys will make them take your request seriously.

There is a funny thing about this meeting though – it really doesn't matter. This person really doesn't have the authority to tell you yes or no. That power is held by the Interfraternity Council (IFC) on campus.

All you want to do is be able to say that you discussed the possibility with the university, and that they were somewhat open to it. As long as the director didn't tell you there is no way in hell, then they are somewhat open to it.

There is a very important reason why you want to check this box...

Picking a National Fraternity

When you start talking to national fraternities, they will ask you two things. First, they will want to know how big your interest group is. If you are anywhere near 20, they will be impressed. Next, they will want to know if you talked to the university. Again, if you have they will be impressed. That is why you talk to the Greek Life director first.

So how do you start the conversations with the national fraternities? First off, narrow your list to four or five. Then, send them an email explaining you have developed an interest group and you are looking to start a fraternity. Let them know you have talked to the university, and they are open to the idea. Then, ask them the following questions:

1) How much are your dues/insurance?
2) What services does the fraternity provide with those fees?
3) What is your process for becoming a chartered chapter?
4) What type of support do you provide a new colony?
5) What makes your fraternity special?

If they answer those couple questions, you should get a good feel for what fraternity is right for you. The last question is especially interesting, because that is open-ended enough that they will be able to give you some really good information about their fraternity.

Also, you will be able to tell a lot from the answers you get back. If someone is detailed, prompt and professional in their response, then that is probably someone you want to work with.

If they give you a form response, then screw them and move on.

Once you pick a fraternity, set up a phone conference to discuss starting a new chapter. If the conversation goes well, the fraternity will send a leadership consultant to your school to help you get the colony started. If it doesn't go well, keep talking to fraternities until you find the right one.

Putting it All Together

At this stage, the national fraternity will start adding value to your relationship by ensuring you get your colony off the ground. They will meet with the university which will add significance to your intentions. They will assist you in meeting with the IFC to get conditional approval. And most importantly, they will help you get your fraternity started off on the right foot.

One Last Step

At this stage, you have more or less started a fraternity. But I do have a bit of sobering information to share. Of the 20 guys who started in your interest group, probably only 10 or so will ever graduate as brothers. Some will get bored with the idea. Others will find out it was too much work and quit. Some will fail out of school. Believe me when I say that probably half will never graduate as brothers.

What I am telling you is that starting a fraternity is essentially a numbers game. If you are going to lose half of your starting group, wouldn't it be easier to start with 60 as opposed to 20? Fortunately, that is easy to do, and this is the second most critical step to your success.

You need to hold an open interest meeting after establishing the initial interest group of 20.

To do so, you must first reserve an auditorium on campus. Take the lists of potential recruits from the 20 guys in the interest group. Email each one of those guys letting them know that you will be starting a fraternity and they were recommended to be a part of it.

Tell them you will be holding a short informational meeting and would love it if they would join. Ask them to email you back if they plan on attending. If they email back, it is much more likely that they will honor their commitment and show up.

Of course, this is the lazy man's way of doing it. It would be much more effective if you actually invited people in person, but I realize time is of the essence.

In addition, make a flyer, and put a couple hundred around campus. Be sure to publicize the meeting on the facebook page of all 20 guys in the interest group. Get the word out that you are starting a fraternity, and that you want everyone who is possibly interested to attend a short meeting to learn more.

At the meeting, explain your vision for the fraternity. Let the guys know what you are going to be about, and why you are starting a new fraternity. Explain to them the thought process of picking the national fraternity you chose.

Hopefully, a representative from nationals will be there, and will be able to help recruit for you.

Realize that for this to be successful you need to let the new guys know that they are getting in on the ground floor. They will be full-fledged founding fathers, and they will have a direct impact on creating the new fraternity. This will be a powerful message and hopefully some guys will be interested.

Finally, be sure to follow up with each person that attended the session a day or two after the interest meeting. You want to gauge their interest.

Your interest group should grow significantly as a result of this meeting. And again, it is a numbers game. The larger the initial group starts out with, the easier it will be to survive the guys who will eventually quit.

Becoming a Chapter

If you have reached this stage, you have had an incredible accomplishment. Remember though that you now essentially have 40 to 60 new members running around with little concept of what the fraternity is all about. You have to keep them engaged at this stage or run the risk of losing them.

Fortunately, all the information you need to know to run a world-class fraternity is on my website. Please use it, and share it with your brothers.

Conclusion

That is it in a nutshell. I know it seems like a ton, but it is just a few really big steps. A couple of motivated guys can accomplish this will very few problems. One important thing I have learned in life is that you can overcome lack of knowledge with superior effort. If you are dedicated to your vision of starting a new fraternity, you will be successful.

ABOUT THE AUTHOR

Pat Daley was initiated into Pi Lambda Phi Fraternity at North Carolina State University in the fall of 1997. He was initiated the weekend after his fraternity was chartered, and was able to see the chapter grow from its infancy.

Pat would go on to become the president of his chapter for two years as well as the IFC president of the university. He was elected to be the Undergraduate Representative to Pi Lambda Phi's International Executive Council. These organizations thrived under his leadership, and he was recognized with the following awards: • Brother of the Year – NC State University Chapter of Pi Lambda Phi • NC State University Fraternity Man of the Year • Rafer Johnson Upsilon Achievement Award – presented to the most outstanding brother nationally in Pi Lambda Phi Fraternity.

Pat launched the thefratenrityadvisro.com in the summer of 2009 and it has been a huge success. Literally thousands of visitors have read his columns. He authored The Fraternity Leader in 2010, which is Pat's best collection of fraternity advice, and is a must-have for any fraternity man.

In 2012 Pat launched howtojoinafraternity.com and wrote How to Join a Fraternity to specifically address one of the most common questions undergraduates ask on thefraternityadvisor.com. His desire is this book and the site help all prospective fraternity men find the right fraternity for them.

Made in the USA
Lexington, KY
23 February 2014